ISBN: 979-8-8693-0828-3

<u>Burnt Toast Saves Marriages</u>
*How Mistakes And Imperfections
Can Strengthen Love And Commitment*

Published by Verse One Enterprises
An imprint of E. Marcel Ministries

www.emarceljones.com

CONTENTS

INTRODUCTION

Imperfection is woven into the very fabric of our being. Since the fall of mankind, we were flawed creatures, subject to the influence of evil and frail in our very nature. Yet, far from being a sign of failure or inadequacy, our imperfections shape us into the individuals we are and provide the platform for our Creator to go to work on our behalf.

In Psalm 138:8, we are reminded of the profound truth that the Lord will perfect that which concerns us. It is a reassurance that even in our imperfection, we are held in the loving embrace of God's mercy and grace. His enduring love and compassion extend to us, flawed and imperfect as we are, and He never forsakes the works of His hands.

As we navigate the complexities of human relationships, we also must recognize that our unions are inherently imperfect. Each of us brings our own unique set of strengths, weaknesses, and idiosyncrasies to the table, shaping the dynamics of our relationships in ways both beautiful and challenging. Yet, it is precisely in our imperfections that the hand of God can be seen most clearly.

God, the Master Tailor, knits together the intricate tapestry of our lives and weaves the threads of our triumphs and failures into a masterpiece of His design. He is the author of our love stories, the architect of our unions, and the guiding force behind our journey toward wholeness and fulfillment. Our marriage is significant only when He has his hand in it.

In the pages that follow, we will explore the profound truth that even in our imperfection, there is beauty to be found. We will delve into the complexities of human relationships, exploring the highs and lows that shape our journey toward deeper love and connection. And through it all, we will seek to uncover the plan of God at work, perfecting that which concerns us and guiding us toward a greater understanding of His enduring love and mercy.

So let us embark on this journey together, embracing our imperfections as a testament to the divine design of our Creator. For in His hands, even the most imperfect unions can be transformed into something beautiful and enduring. And as we journey forward, may we be ever mindful of the words of Psalm 138:8, trusting in the promise that God's mercy endures forever, and that He will perfect that which concerns us.

Dr. E. Marcel Jones

PREACHER • TEACHER • LEADER

CHAPTER 1 – No One Is Perfect

Let's talk relationships, specifically marriages. From the moment we say "I do" at the wedding ceremony, there's an unspoken expectation of perfection. The flawless dress, the picturesque venue, the ideal vows—all contribute to this illusion of a perfect union. But as the honeymoon fades and reality sets in, couples quickly realize that perfection is but a fleeting mirage. He smells! She's moody!He's a mama's boy! She snorts when she laughs! In other words, neither the husband nor the wife is perfect!

Marriages are not built on perfection. In fact, they thrive amidst imperfection. Why? Because marriages don't involve perfect individuals. They bring together two flawed, imperfect beings— hopefully, sound-minded and spiritually whole, but imperfect nonetheless. To expect perfection from either partner is to set oneself up for disappointment and disillusionment. As must as you may have adored your mother, she is not your mother. And, he is not your father. NEWSFLASH – your parents weren't perfect either.

The truth is, imperfection is inherent in all aspects of the marital relationship. From communication breakdowns to disagreements over finances, from struggles with intimacy to differing parenting styles—every aspect of marriage is marked by imperfection. And yet, it is precisely within these imperfections that the true beauty of marriage lies.

When we embrace the reality of our imperfections and acknowledge that they also exist within our relationships, a profound transformation occurs. Instead of striving for an unattainable ideal, we learn to accept and even celebrate our imperfections and we learn to acknowledge, understand, and even accept the imperfections in others, including our spouses. We understand that it's not about finding perfection within our partner or our marriage, but rather about embracing the imperfections that make us human.

So what if she burns the toast every morning. At least she's attempting to contribute to the relationship. It's not a perfect contribution. But it's a contribution, nonetheless. So what if he's loud when he watches sports on the weekend. At least he's at home with the family and not out in the streets chasing other women for sport! Our imperfections can be the gateway to strengthening our marriages.

This revelation opens the door to greater love and deeper commitment. It fosters empathy, compassion, and understanding —qualities that are essential for a thriving marriage. Rather than viewing imperfections as obstacles to be overcome, we see them as opportunities for growth and connection.

In essence, our imperfections shape who we are and the relationships we exist within. They remind us of our humanity and keep us grounded in reality. Far from being the downfall of marriage, our imperfections are the very foundation upon which lasting, fulfilling relationships are built.

It's the imperfections that save our marriages, not destroy them. They teach us patience, resilience, and forgiveness. They remind us that love is not about finding someone perfect, but about accepting someone perfectly imperfect. Ooooooo, that's deep!

So I encourage you to embrace each other's imperfections, both individually and within the marriage. Celebrate the quirks, flaws, and idiosyncrasies that make you who you are. For it is through embracing our imperfections that we find true love, lasting fulfillment, and the beauty of a marriage that stands the test of time. In the pages that follow, allow me to take you on the path to releasing the power and promise of a fulfilling marriage despite the imperfections that are present. Let me explain how burnt toast can save your marriage.

CHAPTER 2 – The Quest For ~~THE PERFECT~~
A Fulfilling Marriage

In the realm of relationships, particularly within the sacred institution of marriage, the pursuit of perfection often looms large. We're bombarded by societal standards and ideals that dictate what a perfect marriage should look like. But what exactly does perfection mean in the context of marriage, and is it even attainable?

Society's definition of perfection is as elusive as it is arbitrary. Whether it's striving for a perfect 10 in gymnastics or seeking out the flawless diamond, the concept of perfection seems to constantly shift and evolve. We're left chasing after an ideal that's ever-changing, making it nearly impossible to grasp.

The truth is, perfection is subjective. What one person deems as perfect may not align with another's definition. This inherent subjectivity makes it challenging to establish a universal standard for perfection. Even when we attempt to quantify perfection objectively, we often fall short in developing the proper criteria.

Thus, it becomes imperative to redefine perfection, especially within the context of marriage. Rather than chasing after an unattainable ideal, we must shift our focus towards a more realistic and sustainable vision of marital perfection.
Within the confines of marriage, there are five key criteria that should be considered when attempting to determine perfection:

1. **Communication:** Effective communication forms the bedrock of a healthy marriage. Perfect communication doesn't mean never disagreeing or arguing, but rather being able to express oneself openly and honestly while listening to and respecting one's partner.

2. **Trust**: Trust is the cornerstone of any successful marriage. Perfect trust doesn't imply blind faith, but rather a deep sense of security and reliability in each other, built through honesty, transparency, and mutual respect.

3. **Respect**: Mutual respect is essential for a harmonious marriage. Perfect respect involves valuing each other's opinions, feelings, and boundaries, even in times of disagreement or conflict.

4. **Support**: A perfect marriage is characterized by unwavering support and encouragement from both partners. This means standing by each other through thick and thin, offering comfort, encouragement, and reassurance when needed.

5. **Growth**: A perfect marriage is one that fosters personal and relational growth. It's about continuously evolving and improving as individuals and as a couple, learning from past mistakes and experiences, and growing stronger together.

By redefining perfection within the bounds of marriage based on these five criteria, we can free ourselves from the unrealistic standards imposed by society. Instead of chasing after an unattainable ideal, we can focus on cultivating a relationship that is grounded in communication, trust, respect, support, and growth.

In conclusion, the pursuit of perfection in marriage is a noble endeavor, but it's essential to redefine what perfection truly means. By shifting our focus towards more realistic and sustainable criteria, we can build marriages that are not only fulfilling but also resilient in the face of life's challenges. It's time to let go of society's arbitrary standards and embrace a new vision of perfection—one that celebrates the beauty of imperfection and the strength of love.

CHAPTER 3 – DANGER DANGER

Imperfections and insecurities can wreak havoc on a marriage if left unchecked. It is essential for couples to address these issues openly and honestly, seeking support from a therapist or counselor if necessary. By fostering trust, communication, and vulnerability, couples can overcome their insecurities and build a stronger, more resilient relationship. Listed in this chapter are 10 Signs that imperfections and insecurities are destroying the fabric of your marriage.

1.   **Lack of Communication**: One of the most significant signs that imperfections and insecurities are damaging your marriage is a breakdown in communication. When you're struggling to openly express your thoughts, feelings, and concerns, it creates a barrier to intimacy and understanding. Insecurities may lead to fear of judgment or rejection, causing your spouse to withhold important information or feelings. Additionally, imperfections may cause defensiveness or avoidance in communication, further exacerbating misunderstandings and conflicts.

2.   **Trust Issues:** Imperfections and insecurities can erode trust in a marriage, leading to suspicion, doubt, and paranoia. When one or both partners struggle with feelings of inadequacy or fear of betrayal, it can manifest in behaviors such as snooping, questioning, or accusing without evidence. Trust issues may stem from past experiences or unresolved insecurities, but they can severely damage the foundation of a marriage if left unaddressed.

3. **Emotional Distance:** Insecurities and imperfections often contribute to emotional distance between partners. When individuals feel insecure about themselves or their relationship, they may withdraw emotionally as a coping mechanism. This emotional distance can manifest as a lack of affection, intimacy, or engagement in meaningful conversations. Over time, the emotional disconnect can lead to feelings of loneliness and isolation within the marriage.

4. **Constant Comparison:** Whichever spouse struggles with insecurities may engage in constant comparison, both internally and externally. He or she may compare himself or herself to the other spouse, feeling inferior or inadequate in comparison to his or her perceived flaws. Similarly, he or she may compare the marriage to others' marriages, feeling envious or resentful of seemingly PERFECT couples. Constant comparison can fuel feelings of insecurity and dissatisfaction, leading to resentment and dissatisfaction within the marriage.

5. **Blame and Criticism:** Imperfections and insecurities may manifest in patterns of blame and criticism within the marriage. When individuals feel insecure about themselves or their relationship, they may project their insecurities onto their partner, criticizing them for perceived flaws or shortcomings. Similarly, they may blame their partner for their own insecurities or unhappiness, deflecting responsibility for their own feelings. Blame and criticism create a toxic cycle of negativity that undermines trust and mutual respect within the marriage.

6. **Escalating Conflict**: Insecurities and imperfections often contribute to escalating conflict within the marriage. When individuals feel insecure or vulnerable, they could become defensive or reactive in response to perceived threats. This can lead to arguments, power struggles, and emotional outbursts that further damage the relationship. Escalating conflict creates a hostile environment that undermines intimacy and undermines the foundation of the marriage.

7. **Avoidance of Vulnerability:** The individual that struggles with insecurities may avoid vulnerability as a way to protect himself or herself from potential pain or rejection. You might witness one spouse withholding his or her true thoughts and feelings, fearing judgment or criticism. Similarly, he or she might avoid discussing sensitive topics or sharing their deepest desires and fears to avoid vulnerability. Unfortunately, avoidance of vulnerability creates a barrier to intimacy and prevents couples from truly connecting on a deeper level.

8. **Self-Sabotage:** Insecurities and imperfections can lead to self-sabotaging behaviors that undermine the health of the marriage. Individuals might engage in self-destructive behaviors such as substance abuse, excessive spending, or infidelity as a way to cope with their insecurities or escape from their problems. Self-sabotage not only harms the individual but also damages the trust and stability of the marriage.

9. **Resentment and Bitterness:** Unresolved insecurities and imperfections often lead to feelings of resentment and bitterness within the marriage as well. When individuals feel misunderstood or unaccepted by their partner, they may harbor resentment towards them, leading to passive-aggressive behavior or emotional withdrawal. Similarly, they might feel bitter towards themselves for their perceived shortcomings, leading to self-loathing or depression. Resentment and bitterness poison the atmosphere of the marriage, making it difficult to foster love and connection.

10. **Loss of Connection:** Ultimately, the most devastating sign that imperfections and insecurities are destroying your marriage is a loss of connection between spouses. When individuals feel insecure or inadequate, it creates a barrier to intimacy and prevents couples from truly connecting spiritually, physically, and emotionally. Without a strong spiritual, physical, and emotional connection, the marriage becomes hollow and unfulfilling, leading to feelings of loneliness and despair.

CHAPTER 4 – So What's Our Plan

In the journey of marriage, one of the most profound and liberating moves a couple can make is to embrace their mistakes and failures. It's an acknowledgment of the reality that neither partner is perfect, and that missteps and failures are not only inevitable but also essential for growth and resilience in the relationship.

Perfection is an elusive goal that no couple can ever truly achieve. With each partner being fallible human beings, it's not a matter of "if" mistakes will occur, but rather "when" they will happen. Instead of fearing or avoiding failure, couples can choose to embrace it as an opportunity for growth and learning.

A powerful way to foster this mindset is through regular reflection and communication within the marriage. One practical strategy is to schedule a monthly date night dedicated to discussing both the successes (GLOWS) and areas for improvement (GROWS) in the relationship. This intentional time allows couples to honestly and judgment-free evaluate their marriage, celebrate their achievements, and address any challenges they may be facing.

During these discussions, it's crucial to create a safe and supportive environment where both partners feel comfortable sharing their thoughts and feelings openly. Honesty, vulnerability, and empathy are key components of effective communication in marriage. By listening to each other's perspectives and experiences, couples can gain valuable insights into their own strengths and weaknesses.

To facilitate these discussions, couples can try using specific discussion starters aimed at reflecting on mistakes and failures and committing to growth together. For example:

1. **Reflect on past mistakes:** Start by sharing a specific mistake or failure that you've experienced in the past month. Discuss what led to the mistake, how it affected you and your partner, and what you've learned from the experience.

2. **Commit to accountability:** Discuss ways in which you can support each other in overcoming challenges and holding each other accountable. This may involve setting specific goals, creating action plans, or establishing regular check-ins to track progress.

3. **Share your vision for growth:** Take turns sharing your vision for how you want to grow individually and as a couple. Discuss the steps you can take to achieve these goals and how you can support each other along the way.

Case studies and real-life examples demonstrate the transformative power of embracing mistakes and failures in marriage. Couples who learn to overcome challenges within themselves often find that their relationship is strengthened, and their marital bonds are reinforced. By navigating through their individual imperfections together, couples can cultivate a deeper understanding, appreciation, and love for each other.

In conclusion, embracing mistakes and failures is not a sign of weakness but rather a testament to the strength and resilience of a marriage. By creating space for open communication, reflection, and growth, couples can turn their challenges into opportunities for deeper connection and intimacy. It's through these shared experiences of triumph and tribulation that couples can truly strengthen their marital bonds and build a relationship that stands the test of time.

CHAPTER 5 – The Power Of The "F" Bomb

Marriage stands as one of the most profound and complex bonds. It is a union of two imperfect beings navigating through life together, both carrying their own set of flaws and imperfections. Yet, it is precisely within these imperfections that the true beauty and strength of a marriage can be found. As couples journey together, they inevitably encounter moments of hurt, disappointment, and frustration. However, it is how they navigate through these challenges that ultimately shapes the course of their relationship. This chapter will explore the profound significance of forgiveness and compassion within the context of marriage, and how they serve as indispensable tools for nurturing a relationship grounded in grace and mercy.

Exploring Imperfections: In every relationship, there comes a point where the rose-tinted glasses of infatuation are replaced by the sobering reality of imperfection. Couples begin to uncover each other's flaws, quirks, and vulnerabilities, sometimes leading to friction and conflict. However, rather than viewing these imperfections as obstacles, they should be seen as opportunities for growth and understanding. Embracing one another's imperfections fosters a deeper sense of empathy and compassion, laying the foundation for a resilient and enduring bond.

Cultivating Forgiveness: Forgiveness is a cornerstone of healthy relationships, especially within the sacred union of marriage. It is the antidote to resentment, bitterness, and grudges that can poison the very fabric of a relationship. Contrary to popular belief, forgiveness does not entail forgetting or excusing the offense; rather, it is a conscious choice to release the burden of anger and resentment. When we extend forgiveness to our spouse, we liberate ourselves from the shackles of negativity and create space for healing and reconciliation.

Forgiveness is a multifaceted gem that shines with the light of grace and mercy. It not only benefits the offender by offering them a chance at redemption but also empowers the offended to reclaim their sense of peace and emotional well-being. By letting go of past hurts and grievances, couples pave the way for deeper intimacy, trust, and connection within their marriage.

Operating with Compassion: In the tumultuous journey of marriage, it is easy to become fixated on our partner's shortcomings and failings. However, beneath the surface of every mistake lies a story of struggle, pain, and vulnerability. Practicing compassion involves seeing beyond the fall and embracing the humanity of our spouse. It requires us to extend empathy, understanding, and support, even in the face of disappointment or frustration.

Compassion acts as a gentle salve that soothes the wounds of the heart and fosters a sense of solidarity and unity within the marriage. By acknowledging and validating each other's experiences, couples cultivate a climate of emotional safety and trust, where vulnerability is celebrated rather than shamed.

Strategies for Cultivating Forgiveness and Compassion: To integrate forgiveness and compassion into the fabric of your marriage, consider employing the following practical strategies:

- Cultivate empathy through active listening and genuine curiosity about each other's perspectives.
- Practice gratitude by focusing on the positive attributes and contributions of your spouse.
- Engage in regular dialogue and conflict resolution to address grievances and misunderstandings.
- Set healthy boundaries to protect the emotional well-being of you both.
- Seek spiritual guidance or professional counseling when you are faced with persistent challenges or unresolved conflicts.

Conclusion: Forgiveness and compassion are the golden threads that bind hearts and souls together. They have the power to transform pain into healing, conflict into understanding, and estrangement into intimacy. As you embark on the journey of marriage, remember that imperfection is not a flaw to be fixed but a canvas to be painted with the colors of forgiveness and compassion. By embracing each other's imperfections and cultivating grace and mercy, together you both can forge a relationship that will withstand the test of time and emerge stronger, wiser, and more resilient than ever before.

CHAPTER 6 – Be HONEST, "Does This Dress Make My…"

Open and honest communication stands as the cornerstone of connection and understanding. Particularly in imperfect relationships, where flaws and shortcomings are inevitable, the ability to acknowledge and address these imperfections is paramount for growth and progress. Yet, in a world where vulnerability is often perceived as weakness and honesty can be uncomfortable, fostering effective communication requires intentionality and skill. In this chapter, we will delve into the significance of open and honest communication in imperfect relationships, exploring the necessity of acknowledging each other's flaws and providing practical techniques for nurturing effective dialogue.

The Importance of Acknowledging Imperfections

In any relationship, whether romantic, familial, or platonic, acknowledging each other's imperfections is crucial for fostering trust, intimacy, and growth. Human beings are inherently flawed, and pretending otherwise only serves to create barriers to genuine connection. By bravely confronting the reality of our imperfections and vulnerabilities, we create a foundation of authenticity and acceptance upon which our relationships can thrive. Moreover, by acknowledging our own shortcomings, we pave the way for empathy and understanding towards our partners, fostering a culture of mutual support and growth.

Assertiveness over Aggressiveness or Passiveness

Effective communication in imperfect relationships requires a delicate balance between assertiveness and sensitivity. Assertiveness entails confidently expressing one's thoughts, feelings, and needs without infringing upon the rights or boundaries of others. It involves speaking up for oneself while also remaining receptive to the perspectives and feelings of our partners. In contrast, aggressiveness involves dominating or belittling others, while passiveness involves avoiding conflict or suppressing one's own needs and desires. By cultivating assertiveness, couples can navigate through challenging conversations with respect, empathy, and integrity, fostering deeper connection and mutual understanding.

Addressing the Elephant in the Room

In many imperfect relationships, there often exists an unspoken tension or issue that looms large but goes unaddressed. This "elephant in the room" can create a sense of unease or disconnection, hindering the growth and progress of the relationship. However, by mustering the courage to confront uncomfortable truths and have difficult conversations, couples can unravel the knots of misunderstanding and resentment, paving the way for healing and resolution. Addressing the elephant in the room requires vulnerability, empathy, and a willingness to lean into discomfort for the sake of growth and connection.

Practical Techniques for Fostering Effective Communication

To cultivate open and honest communication in imperfect relationships, couples can employ a variety of practical techniques. These include:

- *Active Listening:* Practice attentive listening without interruption, judgment, or defensiveness, allowing your partner to express themselves fully and feel heard and understood.
- *Vulnerability:* Share your thoughts, feelings, and vulnerabilities openly and authentically, creating a safe space for emotional intimacy and connection.
- *Nonverbal Communication:* Pay attention to nonverbal cues such as body language, tone of voice, and facial expressions, which can convey unspoken emotions and needs.
- *Empathy:* Put yourself in your partner's shoes, seeking to understand their perspective and feelings with compassion and curiosity.
- *Conflict Resolution:* Approach conflicts as opportunities for growth and understanding, using effective communication techniques such as "I" statements, active listening, and compromise.
- *Regular Check-Ins:* Schedule regular check-ins to discuss the state of your relationship, identify areas for improvement, and reaffirm your commitment to open communication and mutual growth.

In imperfect relationships, open and honest communication serves as a guiding light, illuminating the path towards deeper connection, understanding, and growth. By bravely acknowledging each other's imperfections, cultivating assertiveness, and addressing the elephants in the room, couples can navigate through challenges with grace, empathy, and resilience. Through the practice of active listening, vulnerability, empathy, and conflict resolution, couples can foster a culture of open communication that nourishes the roots of their relationship and allows it to flourish amidst the ebb and flow of life's inevitable imperfections.

CHAPTER 7 – Navigating Our Challenges And Building Resilience

It is often said that knowing is half the battle. Understanding and acknowledging the imperfections and challenges that inevitably arise in any relationship is indeed a crucial first step. However, true growth and meaning in marriage come not from simply recognizing these imperfections, but from actively embracing them and navigating through adversity together. In this chapter, we will explore the transformative power of resilience in marriage, how overcoming challenges can lead to personal and relational growth, and practical strategies for navigating obstacles as a couple.

Embracing Imperfections

Marriage is a mosaic of imperfections, a tapestry woven with the threads of individual quirks, flaws, and vulnerabilities. Rather than striving for an idealized version of perfection, couples must embrace the richness and complexity of their relationship, imperfections and all. It is within these imperfections that the true beauty and depth of a marriage can be found. Embracing imperfections requires a shift in perspective, from seeing flaws as obstacles to seeing them as opportunities for growth and connection. By acknowledging and accepting each other's imperfections, couples create a foundation of authenticity and vulnerability upon which their relationship can flourish.

Navigating Challenges

While imperfections add texture and depth to a marriage, they also bring with them challenges and obstacles. From communication breakdowns to financial struggles to external stressors, couples must navigate through a myriad of challenges together. However, rather than viewing challenges as threats to the stability of their relationship, couples can approach them as opportunities for growth and resilience. The obstacles that often lead some couples to divorce can actually serve as catalysts for deeper intimacy and connection if approached with courage, compassion, and determination.

Building Resilience

Resilience is the ability to bounce back from adversity, to weather life's storms with grace and fortitude. In the context of marriage, resilience is not only a personal attribute but also a relational one. Couples who cultivate resilience are better equipped to navigate through challenges together, emerging stronger and more united on the other side. Resilience fosters personal growth by cultivating qualities such as perseverance, adaptability, and emotional intelligence. It also strengthens the bond between partners, fostering trust, empathy, and mutual support.

Strategies for Navigating Challenges

Navigating challenges as a couple requires intentionality, communication, and collaboration. The following strategies can help couples build resilience and navigate obstacles effectively:

- *Open and Honest Communication:* Create a safe space for open and honest dialogue, where both partners feel heard, understood, and supported.
- *Teamwork:* Approach challenges as a team, working together to identify solutions and support each other through difficult times.
- *Flexibility:* Remain flexible and adaptable in the face of adversity, recognizing that unexpected setbacks are a natural part of life.
- *Self-Care:* Prioritize self-care and emotional well-being, recognizing that taking care of oneself is essential for supporting the relationship.
- *Seek Support:* Reach out for support from friends, family, or professional counselors when needed, recognizing that it is okay to ask for help.
- *Cultivate Gratitude:* Focus on the positive aspects of your relationship, expressing gratitude for each other's strengths and contributions.

Knowing is indeed half the battle. Understanding and acknowledging the imperfections and challenges that arise is a crucial first step. However, true growth and meaning in marriage come from actively embracing these imperfections navigating through adversity together. By embracing imperfections, navigating challenges, and building resilience, couples can foster personal and relational growth, transforming obstacles into opportunities for deeper intimacy, connection, and meaning in their marriage.

CHAPTER 8 – It Depends On Which Side You're Looking At…

My maternal grandmother had a way of turning the most horrible kitchen disaster into a loving meal. I recall the day I decided to help her in the kitchen with preparing breakfast. At the age of 12, my job was simply to butter the toast and place it in the oven for a quick broil. Despite her warnings issued to me several times within a span of 2 minutes, I managed to burn the last of the bread for breakfast that morning. Distraught and feeling like I had disappointed her, my grandmother simply expressed, "It's okay… I've burned a lot of bread in my lifetime."

Taking two pieces of bread into her hands, she rubbed the charred sides against each other while holding them over the sink. When she pulled them apart, all of the black, charred, burnt sections were in the sink and the pieces of bread were golden yellow. I thought she was some sort of magician. But, the reality was that in that moment, my grandmother was teaching me an invaluable lesson about how to deal with imperfect moments in life by finding a way to express gratitude.

In the hustle and bustle of daily life, it's easy for couples to get caught up in the routine of responsibilities and forget to nurture the joy and love in their relationship. While milestone events like anniversaries, job promotions, and graduations are certainly cause for celebration, it's equally important for couples to welcome opportunities to celebrate regularly, even in the midst of life's ordinary moments. Finding joy in marriage requires intentionality and a willingness to embrace the imperfect moments that make up the fabric of everyday life. In this chapter, we will explore the importance of celebrating love and joy in marriage, how embracing imperfections can lead to a deeper sense of gratitude and connection, and practical tips for incorporating regular celebrations into your relationship.

Embracing Imperfect Moments: Marriage is a journey filled with ups and downs, twists and turns, and unexpected detours. It's in the imperfect moments—the squabbles over household chores, the quirky habits that annoy us, the mundane routines of daily life—that the true beauty and richness of marriage can be found. Rather than viewing these imperfections as obstacles to happiness, couples can choose to embrace them as opportunities for growth, understanding, and connection. It's in these imperfect moments that the unique quirks and idiosyncrasies of our partners shine brightest, reminding us of the depth and complexity of love.

Finding Joy in Everyday Moments: Happiness is not a passive state that magically appears at our doorstep every morning; it's a choice that we make each day. Finding joy in marriage requires intentional effort and a commitment to celebrating love and gratitude in even the smallest of moments. Whether it's sharing a cup of coffee in the morning, taking a leisurely stroll hand-in-hand, or simply cuddling on the couch after a long day, couples can find countless reasons to celebrate love and connection in their everyday lives. By cultivating a spirit of appreciation and gratitude, couples can infuse their relationship with joy and meaning, creating a foundation of love that sustains them through life's challenges.

Practical Tips for Regular Celebrations — Incorporating regular celebrations into your relationship doesn't have to be complicated or extravagant. Simple gestures of love and appreciation can have a profound impact on the health and happiness of your marriage. Consider incorporating one of the following practical tips into your weekly interactions with your spouse:

- *Gratitude Journal:* Take a few moments each day to write down something you're grateful for about your partner or your relationship.
- *Weekly Date Night:* Set aside one evening each week for a special date night, whether it's a romantic dinner out or a cozy night in.
- *Random Acts of Kindness:* Surprise your partner with small gestures of love and kindness, such as leaving a love note in their lunch or doing a chore they dislike.
- *Shared Hobbies:* Find activities that you both enjoy and make time to pursue them together, whether it's cooking, hiking, or crafting.
- *Appreciation Rituals:* Take turns expressing appreciation for each other at the end of each day, highlighting something specific that you admire or love about your partner.

- *Mini Celebrations:* Create opportunities to celebrate small victories and milestones, whether it's completing a project together or reaching a personal goal.

Finding joy and reasons to celebrate is a choice that couples must make each day. By embracing the imperfect moments and cultivating a spirit of gratitude and appreciation, couples can infuse their relationship with joy, meaning, and connection. Through regular celebrations and acts of love, couples can create a foundation of love that sustains them through life's challenges and brings them closer together with each passing day.

CHAPTER 9 - Restoring Connection

Trust serves as the cornerstone upon which love, intimacy, and connection are built. However, the journey of marriage is fraught with imperfections, mistakes, and failures that can erode trust and strain the marital bond. While it's essential to acknowledge the negative impact of mistakes and imperfections, it's equally important to recognize that all couples fall short of the mark of perfection. Instead of striving for an unattainable ideal, couples can find common ground in the shared experience of imperfection and work together to rebuild trust and connection in the aftermath of challenges and setbacks. In this chapter, we will explore strategies for examining trust issues that may arise from imperfections within the marriage and outline discussion questions to assist with the process of rebuilding trust through transparency, accountability, and forgiveness.

Navigating Imperfections and Trust Issues: Imperfections are an inherent part of the human experience, and they can manifest in various ways within the context of marriage. From communication breakdowns to lapses in judgment, mistakes and failures can shake the foundation of trust between partners. However, while it may be challenging to rebuild trust after an error is committed or as a result of constant displays of imperfection within the relationship, it is not a lost cause. Couples can take proactive steps to examine trust issues, address underlying concerns, and work towards restoring trust and connection in their marriage.

Strategies for Rebuilding Trust:

- *Open and Honest Communication:* Create a safe and non-judgmental space for both partners to express their thoughts, feelings, and concerns openly. Transparency is essential for rebuilding trust and fostering a deeper understanding of each other's perspectives.
- *Acknowledge and Take Responsibility:* Encourage accountability by acknowledging mistakes and taking responsibility for their impact on the relationship. Avoid defensiveness or blame-shifting, and instead focus on repairing the trust that has been damaged.
- *Establish Boundaries:* Set clear boundaries and expectations within the relationship to prevent future breaches of trust. Discuss and agree upon guidelines for communication, behavior, and decision-making to rebuild a sense of security and stability.
- *Demonstrate Consistency:* Consistency is key to rebuilding trust over time. Demonstrate through actions, not just words, that you are committed to regaining your partner's trust and are willing to make changes to ensure it.
- *Seek Professional Guidance:* Consider seeking support from a couples therapist or counselor who can provide guidance and facilitate productive conversations around trust issues. A neutral third party can help navigate difficult emotions and identify constructive solutions for rebuilding trust.

Discussion Questions for Rebuilding Trust:

- What specific actions or behaviors have contributed to the erosion of trust within our relationship?

  ____

  ____

- How have these trust issues impacted our emotional connection and sense of security in the marriage?

  ____

  ____

- What steps can we take individually and collectively to rebuild trust and strengthen our bond?

  ____

  ____

- How can we cultivate open and honest communication to address trust issues more effectively?

  ____

  ____

- What boundaries can we establish to prevent future breaches of trust and protect the integrity of our relationship?

  ____

  ____

- How can we hold each other accountable for our actions and demonstrate a genuine commitment to rebuilding trust?

  ____

  ____

- What role does forgiveness play in the process of rebuilding trust, and how can we work towards forgiving past mistakes and moving forward?

  ____

  ____

- What support or resources do we need to navigate trust issues more effectively, such as couples therapy or self-help resources?

  ____

  ____

- How can we celebrate progress and milestones along the journey of rebuilding trust, reinforcing our commitment to each other and the relationship?

  ____

  ____

- What long-term strategies can we implement to sustain trust and connection in our marriage, even in the face of future challenges or setbacks?

  ____

  ____

Rebuilding trust in marriage is a challenging but worthwhile endeavor that requires courage, patience, and dedication from both partners. By examining trust issues, fostering open communication, and taking proactive steps towards accountability and forgiveness, couples can lay the groundwork for a stronger, more resilient relationship. May these strategies serve as a roadmap for couples navigating challenges or setbacks in their marriage, guiding them towards a renewed sense of trust, connection, and intimacy.

CHAPTER 10 – The Power of Gratitude In Marriage

Amidst the twists and turns, the highs and lows, one constant remains: the power of gratitude. Gratitude has the remarkable ability to breathe life into the mundane, infuse joy into the ordinary, and strengthen the bonds of love and connection between partners. In the face of imperfections and mistakes that inevitably arise, cultivating a spirit of gratitude is not just beneficial—it is essential for maintaining a positive marital environment. In this chapter, we will explore the profound benefits of expressing appreciation within marriage and provide practical strategies for acknowledging your spouse's strengths and efforts, thereby fostering a culture of gratitude and appreciation in your daily life.

The Benefits of Gratitude in Marriage:

1. *Strengthens Emotional Connection:* Expressing gratitude fosters a deeper emotional connection between partners, enhancing feelings of closeness and intimacy.
2. *Enhances Communication:* Gratitude opens the lines of communication, encouraging couples to express their appreciation for each other openly and authentically.
3. *Promotes Forgiveness:* Gratitude facilitates forgiveness by shifting the focus from grievances to gratitude, fostering empathy and understanding.
4. *Cultivates Resilience:* Gratitude nurtures resilience by fostering a positive outlook and helping couples navigate through challenges with grace and optimism.

5. *Improves Overall Well-Being:* Gratitude has been linked to improved mental and physical health, reducing stress levels and promoting overall well-being.

6. *Strengthens Relationship Satisfaction:* Couples who express gratitude for each other report higher levels of relationship satisfaction and longevity.

7. *Fosters Generosity and Kindness:* Gratitude inspires acts of generosity and kindness, creating a ripple effect of positivity within the marriage and beyond.

8. *Deepens Appreciation:* Regularly expressing gratitude allows couples to deepen their appreciation for each other's strengths, contributions, and efforts.

9. *Creates a Positive Marital Environment:* Gratitude fosters a positive marital environment characterized by love, respect, and mutual support.

10. *Strengthens Commitment:* Gratitude reinforces the commitment between partners, reminding them of the value and importance of their relationship.

Strategies for Cultivating Gratitude:

1. *Daily Appreciation Rituals:* Start or end each day by expressing gratitude for something your spouse said or did that you appreciate. Make this part of your daily and/or evening routine.

2. *Express Affection:* Show physical affection and verbal affirmations to express your gratitude and love for your partner. This could be as simple as a hug.

3. *Keep a Gratitude Journal:* Maintain a journal where you record things you are grateful for about your spouse and your marriage. When you keep an accurate record, you will see just how much or how little you recognize moments of gratefulness.

4. *Practice Active Listening:* Listen attentively to your spouse's thoughts, feelings, and experiences, showing appreciation for their perspective. This particular strategy goes a long way!

5. *Share Small Gestures of Kindness:* Surprise your spouse with small acts of kindness or thoughtful gestures that show your appreciation.This involves knowing your spouse's appetite for affection. Have fun and explore hundreds of ways to be kind towards your spouse.

6. *Celebrate Milestones and Achievements:* Acknowledge and celebrate your spouse's accomplishments, no matter how big or small. At the end of a stressful week or day, this strategy is a highly effective tool.

7. *Schedule Regular Appreciation Check-Ins:* Set aside time each week to express gratitude for specific things your spouse has done or said that you appreciate. Be intentional and guard this time as sacred.

Gratitude is a powerful force that has the potential to transform even the most challenging aspects of marriage into opportunities for growth, connection, and joy. By expressing appreciation for your spouse and your marriage, you can cultivate a culture of gratitude that strengthens the emotional bond between the two of you and fosters a positive marital environment. I pray these strategies serve as a roadmap for couples seeking to infuse their relationship with gratitude and appreciation and create a foundation of love and support that sustains them through life's ups and downs.

CHAPTER 11 – Together We Stand

Marriage is not a solitary journey but a shared adventure between two individuals committed to building a life together. From the moment the words "I Do" are spoken, you and your spouse embarked on a journey filled with highs and lows, as well as triumphs and challenges. However, nothing will ever be accomplished in your marriage unless both of you are willing to journey together, hand in hand, as a team. In this chapter, we will explore the importance of teamwork in marriage, the power of embracing imperfections, and several practical strategies for navigating the ups and downs of married life as a united front.

The Importance of Teamwork

In the game of marriage, teamwork is the key to success. No matter how skilled or committed you or your spouse may be, the true strength of your marriage lies in the collective efforts of both partners working together toward common goals. From making major life decisions to tackling everyday challenges, you must approach every aspect of your marriage as a team, supporting and uplifting each other through thick and thin. When you cultivate a spirit of collaboration, communication, and mutual respect, you can navigate through life's uncertainties and challenges with grace and resilience.

Embracing Imperfections

Imperfections exist in every living creature, and nowhere is it more apparent than in the context of marriage. Rather than viewing imperfections as shortcomings to be fixed or hidden, couples can choose to embrace them as opportunities for growth, understanding, and connection. It's through embracing imperfections that couples deepen their love and commitment to each other, recognizing that it's the rough edges and quirks that make their relationship unique and beautiful. By embracing imperfections as a pathway to deeper love and stronger commitment, couples increase their chances of weathering any storm that may come their way.

Practical Strategies for Navigating Challenges

Navigating your marriage as a team requires intentionality, communication, and a willingness to work together through the inevitable challenges and obstacles that arise. Here are some practical strategies for couples to navigate challenges as a united front:

- *Open and Honest Communication:* Create a safe space for open and honest dialogue, where both partners feel heard, understood, and supported.
- *Shared Goals and Values:* Identify common goals and values that you both share and work together to align your actions and decisions accordingly.

- *Division of Responsibilities:* Divide household responsibilities and tasks equitably, taking into account each partner's strengths, preferences, and commitments.
- *Mutual Support:* Offer each other unwavering support and encouragement, especially during times of stress or difficulty.
- *Seek Professional Help:* Don't hesitate to seek professional counseling or support if needed, recognizing that asking for help is a sign of strength, not weakness.
- *Celebrate Small Victories:* Take time to celebrate the small victories and milestones along the way, recognizing and appreciating each other's contributions to the relationship.

As couples journey through the ups and downs of married life, it's essential to remember that nothing will be accomplished unless both partners are willing to embark on this journey together, as a team. By embracing imperfections, communicating openly, and supporting each other through challenges, couples can strengthen their bond, deepen their love, and build a marriage that stands the test of time. May God bless your union and may you find joy in the years to come, embracing even the burnt toast moments as a reminder of the imperfect beauty of marriage lived as a team.

BONUS CHAPTER: Stories of Resilience and Growth

In a world that often glorifies perfection and idealized notions of love, the concept of imperfect love can seem counterintuitive. However, the truth is that imperfection is an inherent part of the human experience, and it is within the realm of imperfection that the most profound and transformative love stories unfold. In this bonus chapter, we will explore the idea of imperfect love through the lens of real-life scenarios and stories of couples who have embraced imperfection and found deeper love and commitment in their marriages. Additionally, we will draw inspiration from the words of wisdom and encouragement shared by relationship experts and mentors, highlighting the beauty and strength of imperfect love.

Stories of Resilience and Growth:

Sarah and James: Sarah and James had been married for over a decade when James lost his job unexpectedly. Instead of allowing this setback to divide them, they came together as a team, supporting each other through the challenges of unemployment. Through their shared struggles, they deepened their bond and rediscovered the strength of their love.

Maria and David: Maria and David faced infertility issues early in their marriage, leading to feelings of disappointment and frustration. Despite the heartache, they remained steadfast in their commitment to each other, leaning on each other for support and finding hope in the midst of adversity. Ultimately, they chose to adopt, and their journey to parenthood strengthened their marriage in unexpected ways.

John and Emily: John and Emily had their fair share of disagreements and misunderstandings throughout their marriage. Instead of letting these moments drive them apart, they learned to communicate openly and honestly, finding common ground and compromise in the face of conflict. Their willingness to embrace imperfection brought them closer together and laid the foundation for a lasting partnership.

Quotes of Wisdom and Encouragement:

"Love isn't about finding someone perfect; it's about finding someone who's perfect for you." - Unknown

"Imperfect love is still worth fighting for because it's real, it's authentic, and it's yours." - Dr. Brené Brown

"Love isn't always perfect. It isn't a fairytale or a storybook. And it doesn't always come easy. Love is overcoming obstacles, facing challenges, fighting to be together, holding on, and never letting go." - Unknown

"Love is not about perfection. It's about embracing each other's imperfections and choosing to love anyway." - Unknown

"The most beautiful thing about imperfect love is that it gives us the opportunity to grow, to learn, and to become better versions of ourselves together." - Unknown

"True love doesn't mean being flawless; it means being willing to work through the flaws together." - Unknown

"Imperfect love is the most genuine and enduring kind of love because it's built on acceptance, forgiveness, and unwavering commitment." - Unknown

Imperfect love is not a flaw to be corrected or a problem to be solved; it is a beautiful and authentic expression of the human experience. Through the stories of couples who have embraced imperfection and the wisdom shared by relationship experts and mentors, we are reminded that imperfection is not a barrier to love but rather a pathway to deeper connection, resilience, and growth. May these reflections serve as a source of inspiration and encouragement for couples navigating the ups and downs of marriage, reminding them that imperfect love is indeed the most beautiful kind of love of all.

MORE BONUS MATERIAL
& Workbook Pages

An IMPERFECT List of IMPERFECTIONS

This checklist serves as a starting point for couples to identify and acknowledge the imperfections present in their marriage. By recognizing and addressing these areas of concern, couples can work towards building a stronger, more resilient relationship based on understanding, communication, and mutual support. Check all that you have observed or display.

COMMUNICATION

- Lack of effective communication
- Communication breakdowns
- Constant misunderstandings
- Difficulty expressing thoughts & feelings
- Unresolved conflicts or disagreements

TRUST

- Trust issues from past betrayals
- Doubt or suspicion regarding spouse's actions
- Holding grudges for long period of time
- Mostly operating independently
- Difficulty rebuilding trust after a breach

INTIMACY

- Lack of emotional intimacy
- Decreased physical intimacy
- Sexual dissatisfaction
- Difficulty expressing affection
- Inability to connect on a deeper level

CONFLICT RESOLUTION

- Inability to resolve conflicts in a healthy manner
- Pattern of repetitive arguments
- Minor disagreements that balloon into major
- Avoidance of conflict or confrontation
- Display of passive-aggression/aggression

An **IMPERFECT** List of **IMPERFECTIONS**

This checklist serves as a starting point for couples to identify and acknowledge the imperfections present in their marriage. By recognizing and addressing these areas of concern, couples can work towards building a stronger, more resilient relationship based on understanding, communication, and mutual support. Check all that you have observed or display.

FINANCIAL

- Financial disagreements or conflicts
- Different financial priorities or spending habits
- Lack of financial security due to past breach
- Financial stress
- Display of indifference as it pertains to money

TIME MANAGEMENT

- imbalance in time spent together versus apart
- Difficulty prioritizing quality time as a couple
- Feeling overwhelmed by busy schedules
- Constant conflicting commitments
- Frustrated whenever shared time is requested

EMOTIONAL SUPPORT

- Lack of emotional support in stressful times
- Inability to empathize with spouse's emotions
- Indifferent toward spouse's past experiences
- Feeling emotional disconnected or distant
- Failure to identify spouse's love language

HOUSEHOLD RESPONSIBILITIES

- Imbalance in division of household duties
- Resentment over imbalance of responsibilities
- Difficulty coordinating tasks
- Failure to complete shared responsibilities
- Neglect of responsibilities altogether

 WWW.EMARCELJONES.COM

An IMPERFECT List of IMPERFECTIONS

This checklist serves as a starting point for couples to identify and acknowledge the imperfections present in their marriage. By recognizing and addressing these areas of concern, couples can work towards building a stronger, more resilient relationship based on understanding, communication, and mutual support. Check all that you have observed or display.

PARENTING
- Obvious differences in parenting styles
- Conflicts over disciplining decisions
- Feeling unsupported in parenting roles
- Imbalance of responsibilities in child-rearing
- Feeling overwhelmed with responsibilities

EXTERNAL INFLUENCES
- Interference from family members
- Lack of barriers to prevent external pressures
- Comparison to other couples
- Strong desire to meet societal expectations
- Work/life stressors impacting marriage

PERSONAL GROWTH
- Struggles with personal growth
- Failure to see the need for self-improvement
- Feeling stagnant or unfulfilled in aspirations
- Lack of personal goal setting
- Difficulty supporting spouse's growth journey

PAST BAGGAGE
- Lingering effects of past trauma
- Unresolved issues hugely impacting behaviors
- Difficulty letting go of past hurts
- Failure to effectively process past resentments
- Refusal to acknowledge need for counseling

An IMPERFECT List of IMPERFECTIONS

This checklist serves as a starting point for couples to identify and acknowledge the imperfections present in their marriage. By recognizing and addressing these areas of concern, couples can work towards building a stronger, more resilient relationship based on understanding, communication, and mutual support. Check all that you have observed or display.

UNREALISTIC EXPECTATIONS
- Pressure to meet individual standards
- Bar for expectations of marriage is unrealistic
- Disappointment when reality falls short
- Difficulty accepting spouse's imperfections
- Indifferent towards spouse's limitations

SPIRITUAL MATURITY
- Strong differences in religious beliefs
- Conflicting religious practices
- Struggles with finding spiritual connection
- Misaligned belief system
- Disconnected from shared spiritual values

EMOTIONAL HEALTH
- Mental health challenges impacting the couple
- Difficulty managing stress within the marriage
- High levels of anxiety and/or depression
- Impact of emotional trauma is heavy
- Intentional avoidance to maintain peace

CULTURAL DIFFERENCES
- Conflicts arising from cultural differences
- Inability to understand/respect backgrounds
- Challenges with navigating cultural traditions
- Feeling misunderstood or unsupported
- Loss of cultural identity to maintain peace

 WWW.EMARCELJONES.COM

BURNT TOAST
Saves Marriages

SELF-IMPROVEMENT WORKSHEET

1
Response

Identify one area of communication in your relationship that you would like to improve.

2

Set a specific goal for enhancing communication (e.g., "I will actively listen to my partner without interrupting").

3

List three actionable steps you can take to improve communication in this area.

BURNT TOAST
Saves Marriages

SELF-IMPROVEMENT WORKSHEET

1   **Response**

- Reflect on any trust issues or concerns that may be present in your relationship.

2

Consider how past experiences may be impacting your ability to trust your partner.

3

Brainstorm strategies for rebuilding trust or strengthening trust in your relationship.

BURNT TOAST
Saves Marriages

SELF-IMPROVEMENT WORKSHEET

1   **Response**

Evaluate the level of emotional and physical intimacy in your relationship.

2

Identify any barriers or challenges to intimacy that you may be experiencing.

3

Set goals for enhancing intimacy (e.g., "I will prioritize quality time with my partner").

BURNT TOAST
Saves Marriages

SELF-IMPROVEMENT WORKSHEET

1

Response

Reflect on your typical approach to resolving conflicts in your relationship.

2

Identify any patterns or recurring issues in your conflict resolution process.

3

Explore new strategies or techniques for resolving conflicts more effectively.

BURNT TOAST
Saves Marriages

SELF-IMPROVEMENT WORKSHEET

1   Response

Review your current financial
situation and identify any areas of
concern or stress.

2

Set financial goals for your
relationship (e.g., saving for a
vacation, paying off debt).

3

Create a budget or financial plan to
help you achieve your financial
goals.

INCOME =

TOTAL DEBT =

MISC SPENDING =

SAVINGS GOAL =

MONTLY SPENDING GOAL =

BURNT TOAST
Saves Marriages

SELF-IMPROVEMENT WORKSHEET

1   **Response**

Assess how you currently manage
your time as a couple.

2

Identify any time management
issues or challenges you may be
facing.

3

Implement time management
strategies (e.g., setting priorities,
scheduling regular date nights).

BURNT TOAST
Saves Marriages

SELF-IMPROVEMENT WORKSHEET

1   **Response**

Reflect on how you and your
partner provide emotional support
to each other.

2

Consider areas where you may be
able to offer more support or
validation.

3

Discuss ways to strengthen
emotional support in your
relationship.

BURNT TOAST
Saves Marriages

SELF-IMPROVEMENT WORKSHEET

1   **Response**

Review the division of household chores and responsibilities in your relationship.

2

Discuss any areas of imbalance or dissatisfaction with your current arrangement.

3

Collaboratively develop a plan for more equitable distribution of household tasks.

BURNT TOAST
Saves Marriages

SELF-IMPROVEMENT WORKSHEET

1

Response

Reflect on your parenting styles and
approaches as a couple.

2

Identify any areas of disagreement
or conflict related to parenting.

3

Explore ways to better support each
other as parents and align your
parenting strategies.

BURNT TOAST
Saves Marriages

SELF-IMPROVEMENT WORKSHEET

1   **Response**

Consider the impact of external
factors (e.g., family, friends, societal
pressures) on your relationship.

2

Identify any external influences that
may be causing stress or tension in
your relationship.

3

Discuss boundaries or strategies for
managing external influences more
effectively.

BURNT TOAST
Saves Marriages

SELF-IMPROVEMENT WORKSHEET

1   **Response**

Reflect on your individual goals and
aspirations for personal growth.

2

Consider how your personal growth
journey may impact your
relationship.

3

Discuss ways to support each
other's personal growth and
development.

BURNT TOAST
Saves Marriages

SELF-IMPROVEMENT WORKSHEET

1   **Response**

Reflect on any past experiences or traumas that may be impacting your relationship.

2

Consider how past baggage may be affecting your ability to fully engage in your relationship.

3

Explore ways to address and heal from past baggage together.

BURNT TOAST
Saves Marriages

SELF-IMPROVEMENT WORKSHEET

1   **Response**

Reflect on any unrealistic
expectations you may have for
yourself or your partner.

2

Consider how these expectations
may be contributing to
dissatisfaction or conflict in your
relationship.

3

Challenge and reframe unrealistic
expectations to promote more
realistic and healthy relationship
dynamics.

BURNT TOAST
Saves Marriages

SELF-IMPROVEMENT WORKSHEET

1   **Response**

Reflect on your shared spiritual
beliefs or practices as a couple.

2

Consider how your relationship with
God plays a role in your relationship
with your spouse and your overall
well-being.

3

Explore ways to deepen your
spiritual connection as a couple.

BURNT TOAST
Saves Marriages

SELF-IMPROVEMENT WORKSHEET

1   Response

Assess your individual emotional
health and well-being.

2

Identify any areas of emotional
struggle or difficulty you may be
experiencing.

3

Discuss strategies for prioritizing
and nurturing your emotional health
as individuals and as a couple.

BURNT TOAST
Saves Marriages

SELF-IMPROVEMENT WORKSHEET

1   **Response**

Reflect on any cultural differences or
backgrounds that may influence
your relationship.

2

Consider how cultural differences
contribute to your relationship
dynamics.

3

Explore ways to celebrate and
honor cultural differences while
fostering understanding and
connection.

Dr. E. Marcel & Tressa Jones

ABC Dating

For Couples

A Guide To Creative Date Nights

For more great inspiration
Check out Dr. E. Marcel Jones' website

www.emarceljones.com

www.ingramcontent.com/pod-product-compliance
Lightning Source LLC
Chambersburg PA
CBHW040132150726
48005CB00015B/2474